CW00520706

Safest

Also by Michael Donaghy

Conjure

Dances Learned Last Night:
Poems 1975–1995

MICHAEL DONAGHY

Safest

PICADOR

First published 2005 by Picador
an imprint of Pan Macmillan Ltd
Pan Macmillan, 20 New Wharf Road, London N1 9RR
Basingstoke and Oxford
Associated companies throughout the world
www.panmacmillan.com

ISBN 0 330 44051 9

Copyright © Michael Donaghy 2005
'A note on title and content' copyright © Maddy Paxman 2005

The Estate asserts on behalf of Michael Donaghy his right
to be identified as the author of this work in accordance
with the Copyright, Designs and Patents Act 1988.

All rights reserved. No part of this publication may be
reproduced, stored in or introduced into a retrieval system, or
transmitted, in any form, or by any means (electronic, mechanical,
photocopying, recording or otherwise) without the prior written
permission of the publisher. Any person who does any unauthorized
act in relation to this publication may be liable to criminal
prosecution and civil claims for damages.

1 3 5 7 9 8 6 4 2

A CIP catalogue record for this book is available from
the British Library.

Typeset by Macmillan Design Department
Printed and bound in Great Britain by
Mackays of Chatham plc, Chatham, Kent

A note on title and content

'Safest' is the name of the computer file in which Michael had stored the poems towards his next collection. On the day he was taken into hospital, although we had very little time before he lost consciousness, he told me that these were the poems he wanted published. I don't know whether he had intended this as the book's title (previous folders were called 'Safe' and 'Safer'), or if it was simply a way of keeping track. But 'Safest' seemed somehow appropriate, and as near as we could get to a title he'd chosen himself.

As to the manuscript, we used only the poems he had selected, resisting the temptation to put back in those he had previously rejected, or include material not yet finished. The exception to this is the fragment of a longer poem about Chief Francis O'Neill, which would I know have been in the book had he lived to complete it – it was a project dear to his heart.

MADDY PAXMAN, 7th May 2005

But the Duende – where is the Duende? Through the empty arch enters a mental air blowing insistently over the heads of the dead, seeking new landscapes and unfamiliar accents; an air bearing the odour of child's spittle, crushed grass, and the veil of a Medusa announcing the unending baptism of all newly created things.

LORCA

Contents

Safest

— I —

In dancing, a single step, a single movement of the body that is graceful and not forced, reveals at once the skill of the dancer. A singer who utters a single word ending in a group of four notes with a sweet cadence, and with such facility that he appears to do it quite by chance, shows with that touch alone that he can do much more than he is doing.

CASTIGLIONE, *The Book of the Courtier*

Upon A Claude Glass

A lady might pretend to fix her face,
but scan the room inside her compact mirror –

so gentlemen would scrutinize this glass
to gaze on Windermere or Rydal Water

and pick their way along the clifftop tracks
intent upon the romance in the box,

keeping unframed nature at their backs,
and some would come to grief upon the rocks.

Don't look so smug. Don't think you're any safer
as you blunder forward through your years

squinting to recall some fading pleasure,
or blinded by some private scrim of tears.

I know. My world's encircled by this prop,
though all my life I've tried to force it shut

The Whip

after Lu Chi (261–303)

Sometimes your writing's a soft tangle of subtleties
undercutting one another, blurring the paths
and you arrive at a washed-out bridge or rockslide.
Leave it. Don't try to end what's finished.
The well-aimed phrase is a whip, your poem a horse,
stamping and snorting and straining at the bit.
He wants to win as much as you do, and the whip
will serve better than a web of fine thoughts.
Just make sure you know when you've won.

I Hold in my Hand an Egg

I hold it aloft between finger and thumb
Like a quail's only smaller, unspeckled.
Be careful, you say, don't drop it.
It may be the egg of the threatened pygmy ghost owl,
and you have broken the law by removing it.

Or *Go on*, you may say, *turn it into a dart,*
or a minnow, a mainspring, a match aflame,
or make it disappear entirely
like that thought I had moments ago
before you began speaking.

Or *No*, you may say, *leave it.*
This egg is replete with meaning.
It is the egg of itself, its own egg,
the philosopher's breakfast.
And you are the Buddha.

Or you may rise and take up arms,
having recognized the egg as *hope*
and my gesture as the signal to an armed cell,
a gesture to be danced or cast in bronze one day.
And I have broken the law by performing it.

Hazards

Once upon a time there was a dark blue suit.
And one fine morning the chamberlain laid it out upon a bed
and the ministers of state assembled round it singing
God preserve and protect the emperor!

2

Don't worry. I gave the dancing monkey your suicide note.
Was it something important? How was I to know?
He's probably torn it to pieces by now or eaten it
or substituted every word for one adjacent in the dictionary.

3

And suddenly there came a sound from heaven as of a rushing
                                        mighty wind,
and cloven tongues like as of fire sat upon the heads of the disciples
and they began to speak with other tongues
in order to confound the multitude.

4

Was it the white pine face like a new moon?
The wet splutter and moan of the shakuhachi?
Was it the actor's dispersal in gesture and smoke?
What part of Noh did you not understand?

The apparatus

What was that exquisite name,
Could I but reach and touch it?
    The hand arranging beads across
Her cold hand in the casket.

Where is that gentle token
By which I tell my love?
    This unopened envelope,
This single empty glove.

She was my lover when we met
How could I betray her?
    The stillness in the photograph
Of a raging river.

Where are the tools by which I map
These planetary motions?
    They come and go beyond your reach.
They make their own decisions.

Who is my accuser?
Who keeps watch all afternoon?
    A glass eye, in a locked drawer,
In a forgotten room.

A Darkroom

I want to keep Klein in this red dark,
and the rawness in my nose and throat.
I want to stay apprenticed to his trade
and I require your assistance.
He's showing me his mother and five sisters
burning back from nothing, fixing them.
I want to come back to this now and again.
I want to retain Klein in the lamp's glare
at his bench, spilling tea, his twenty-minute
emphysema bark, the lung's soft whistle
through the acrid evening to closing up.
I need him to explain this process clearly,
keep him squinting through a jeweller's eyepiece
tinting and retouching faces caught in marriage.
A watchmaker's finesse: ultraviolet irises,
an undertaker's repertoire: rose cheeks
and bloody lips. And here, along his arm –
though my mother's warned me not to stare –
I need to keep them there, the numbers,
crude and blue and blurred and not consecutive,
and keep that ghost who never meets my eye,
his wife, their mad son's shaky scribbles home
in the faint grey blunted pencil they allow him,
read out, wept over, locked back in their strongbox ark,
Klein ramming a broom at the ceiling to silence
the whore who works the cops above his studio,
his sickening breath, but now *I talk too much*
and now it's late, late, and your people will be worried
and as I leave he switches on the light.
I need your help to make that sharp
before it blurs or burns itself to random

as the radio gets tuned to rapid deafening ads,
baseball scores in Spanish, or static, and the dog snarls,
the chain clatters at the door slammed shut behind me.

– II –

And it shall come to pass in the last days, saith God, I will pour out of my Spirit upon all flesh: and your sons and your daughters shall prophesy, and your young men shall see visions, and your old men shall dream dreams: And on my servants and on my handmaidens I will pour out in those days of my Spirit; and they shall prophesy: And I will shew wonders in heaven above, and signs in the earth beneath; blood, and fire, and vapour of smoke: The sun shall be turned into darkness, and the moon into blood, before the great and notable day of the Lord come.

From The Safe House

I can just see Claire your good wife reading you this.
It has arrived this morning at your orchard in Vera Cruz
where your four brown daughters hector six chickens
and you lie beneath the dusty blue pickup
tying back the exhaust with a rusty hanger,
getting ready for the long haul north.

There are parts she skips, parts about her.
And parts I've yet to write or find a way to write.
The paper she reads from is yellowed, sharp-creased,
badly typed, postmarked Chicago, decades late,
from a Reagan winter, Pax Americana for Grenada,
the coldest winter of the life of the mind.

Soon I'll climb through snowdrifts to post it
from our clapboard student commune on the South Side
on a night six mummies dug from permafrost
huddle in coats breathing clouds in a room of books,
watching the last chair leg gutter on the grate
towards the heat death of its universe.

But for now it's still flickering, and Claire is beside me.
I'm too cold to talk, too cold to think, except of her.
I hear you hammer the ice from your boots on the porch
and the door slams back and you blow in from Urbana
from over the lake, from marching with steelworkers.
You look at the fire, the bookshelves, and make the first move.

Four highlighted copies of *One Dimensional Man*,
old phone books, *Jaws*, *The Sensuous Woman* by J.
She's the first shovelled into the fire. You find it now,
hidden behind her, mimeographed, its staples gone to rust,
urgent and crumbly as this letter Claire's holding:
the Manual of the Weather Underground.

We'd been a safe house since '68 and never knew.
Did the Feds? Claire lets go my hand, takes it from you
and sniffs. Could it be any colder there?
Lit by flaring paperbacks and tequila she reads us,
like a bedtime story, the drill for evasion and escape.
I enclose it, with some photos of my son.

I have sent them you *then*, to the farm you planned,
to the heat haze in which you seem to waver,
where you lie beneath the same unsteerable wreck
your wife taught me to drive when you were drunk
and which I still own a seventh of, let's not forget,
(Tell him we never slept together, Claire)

instead of *now*, when I hear of your death,
after your stroke at my age give a month or two,
now, when you never made it to Mexico
and Claire remarried and never had children
and the clapboard safe house fell down at last
and the blue pickup went for scrap years back.

Music Sounds and Helen Passeth over the Stage

stage direction, 'The Tragicall History of Dr. Faustus'

Fireworks crackle and the groundlings gasp and cough
and a drag queen in stiff brocade and starched ruff
glides across the stage on a starry trolley drawn by ropes.
Puppet. Hellbait. Tricktrap. Doctor, wait! She isn't real.
You're doing all the work. She has no lines –
all smoke and candlelight and burning towers.
Not that peerless dame of Greece, this poxy boy
dangling beneath a spangly sky in Rotherhithe
this thirtieth winter of Elizabeth. Curtain.

High summer. Locusts chirrup in the scrub.
Gongs. Ægypt. Enter: Athenian actor chanting
My name is Helen and I will now recount my sorrows.
The gods abducted her, she claims, and sent to Troy
an eidolon of cloud, desire, and big big trouble.
Nobody believes her but they let themselves believe,
these citizens gazing, like adulterous lovers,
through rushlight, moths and incense
toward the still eyes in the white mask.

Look up. Here she is with me up in the gods!
She came to me in tears. What could I do?
I've just been telling her, poor child, she's not to blame.
For just as the owl plummets down, talons wide for the fieldmouse,
just as the drowned are conveyed by the tides to their homes,
such are the whims of the gods and the long views of generals,
such is our nakedness helplessness innocence hubris etcetera.
And she's been pointing out the players for me
having brightened somewhat.

Angelus Novus

As in this amateur footage of a lynch mob when someone hoists a
metal folding chair and commences to batter the swinging corpse
even as others hack at its limbs with machetes, just so Achilles, his
frenzy a runaway train, yokes up his team and drags Hector's carcass
around and around like . . . Stop. Rewind.

Hector dying on his knees in the dust whispering *Prove you're a
man, then, swear by your soul, swear by your gods you won't feed
my corpse to your dogs.*

Fuck you spits Achilles. Freeze frame. Mid-blink, Hector looks into
Achilles' eyes and takes all the time in the world to recall his last
embrace of Andromache and, it hardly now surprises him, to look
back at the future advancing behind him, to his own father
kissing the hands of this killer, the monster taking Priam's hand and
weeping with him, the sound of their sobbing filling the camp. Play
on. Hector's face slams to the dust.

Try to look at this: blind flash victims. Nagasaki. In their endless
1945 they face the camera as unaware of the photographer as they
are of you, viewer. Just so, rage-blind Achilles cannot now glimpse in
Hector's eyes, just before they empty, the terrible pity.

Guilt Wasn't Why She Was Weeping

Like the searchlights that glare through the nursery's breathmisted
                                                    window,
like the static that rasps through the speakers submerging the warning,
like the heat haze of summer that ripples the level horizon,
just so did Helen
take silvery veils on her shoulders.

And she walked the wall weeping where Priam was eyeing up targets.
Then, like a warrior taking his fieldglasses, softly
Priam called out to her, Helen, come sit with me, daughter
kissing her tears away
whispering, Child, don't take on so.

But she threw off his hand – guilt wasn't why she was weeping –
and that whisper she answered with flashed like a silvery spearpoint,
like the static that rasps through the speakers submerging the warning,
like the heat haze of summer
that ripples the level horizon.

Disquietude

Would you know it if our phone was tapped?
Would you hear a series of clicks, for example?
Or the sound of breathing? Or policemen typing?
After the next caller hangs up stay on the line.
Stay on until you're sure.

One day when we were younger and hornier
I stashed a tape recorder underneath our bed. Please don't be angry.
I wanted to keep the noises we were when we weren't ourselves,
but all the mic picked up was wheezing springs. Just as well.
It would be like listening to strangers now.

Our names have sounds besides the ones we hear.
Sometimes, when I wake beside you in the night
and the door of sleep slams shut and locks behind me,
I hear it creep up out of silence, a brash hush,
a crowded emptiness, the static of the spheres.

It's like a tap left on. But it's my own warm blood,
the flood that's washing all the names away,
of schoolmates, kings, the principal export of somewhere,
and all the sounds as well – a lullaby, a child's voice –
my own warm blood that must be blessed.

No recording devices are allowed in this hall.
The lights dim, and onstage they're coughing,
turning pages, giving the score their indivisible attentions,
getting settled for the next movement
which features no one and is silent.

The Moko

Muscles of silence are rolling miles offshore at night,
and each an unpraised perfect wave
cresting this morning in this half-curtained room.
Nothing so dear as these should be so lost.
As any change in the true wind
will show its fingerprint in the sea,
a fresh train of ripples or waves will run
a web over waves caused by the true wind.
Singing. Log drumming. Steering roughly
north by stern bearings of the Southern Cross –
the islands are high and the clouds hover over them.
Nothing so dear as these should be forgotten.
Look on these faces tattooed with maelstroms,
branching fern fronds, with the wave's own codes.
Look on these faces and remember the webbed
imponderables of whirls and eddies.
Observe the cheek spirals – doubly inscribed
tracking the Sun inward to the centre,
the solstice, where it turns and edges
toward the Equinoctial bridge of the nose,
then on to the opposite side of the face.
Moonrise. Watch as a face turns leeward,
for any change in the true wind
will show its fingerprint in the sea.
They knew the stars and steered by singing them
and when the stars were dark, by wind,
and when the winds died, by wave swell,
bird flight, swirled shoals of luminous algae,
by phosphorescence a fathom under the outrigger.
By the million dust motes whorled in the sun shaft,
by every word adrift we whisper in this bed,

they might have sung where we've no skill to reckon.
And nothing of this could have been foreseen.
And nothing so dear as this should be forsaken.

— III —

Norton's Manner

Norton could swallow a number of half-grown frogs and bring them up alive. I remember his anxiety on one occasion when returning to his dressing-room; it seems he had lost a frog – at least he could not account for the entire flock – and he looked very much scared, probably at the uncertainty as to whether or not he had to digest a live frog. At these October Fests I saw a number of frog-swallowers, and to me they were very repulsive indeed. In fact, Norton was the only one I ever saw who presented his act in a dignified manner.

HARRY HOUDINI

Poem On The Underground

Sirs, as ancient maps imagine monsters
so London's first anatomical charts
displayed the innards of a vast loud animal;
writhing discrete circulatory systems
venous, arterial, lymphatic, rendered
into District, Piccadilly, Bakerloo . . .
But Harry Beck's map was a circuit diagram
of coloured wires soldered at the stations.
It showed us all we needed then to know,
and knew already, that the city's
an angular appliance of intentions, not
the blood and guts of everything that happens.
Commuters found it 'easier to read'.

My new 3D design improves on Beck,
restoring something of the earlier complexity.
See, here I've drawn the ordinary lines
but crossing these, weaving through the tunnels,
coded beyond the visible spectrum, I've graphed
the vector of today's security alert
due to a suspect package at Victoria,
to the person under a train at Mill Hill East,
with all the circumstantial stops between.

So the vomiting temp in the last train out of Brixton
links to the fingerless busker doing card tricks
making himself invisible to a crowded carriage.
The lines along the third dimension indicate
connections through time: here, the King's Cross fire
leads back to wartime bivouacs on station platforms
and further still, to children singing on a sunlit hill.
Admittedly my design is less accessible than Beck's,
being infinite and imperceptible, but I'm confident,
that given time, the public would embrace it.
I strongly urge the panel to consider my proposal.
Respectfully submitted, May 9, 2003.

Fragment

Irish Folk Music: A Fascinating Hobby,
With Some Account of Related Subjects,
by Police Chief Francis O'Neill, Chicago, 1910

Any change in the true wind
will show its fingerprint in the sea.
A fresh train of ripples or waves will run
a web over waves caused by the true wind.

   I am the foam on the wave
   I am the bright wave on the white sand
   I am a foredeck gorilla
   I am a lost shoe at a crossroads dance,
if anyone asks. *Still*, you may enquire,
with so few natural attributes,
why did he not stay on land?

After our rescue rations were necessarily limited almost to
starvation. One of the Kanakas had a fine flute, on which he
played a simple one-strain hymn with conscious pride
almost every evening.

Steering roughly
north by stern bearings of the Southern Cross –
the islands are high and the clouds hover over them.
They knew the stars and steered by singing them
and when the stars were dark
they steered by wind and when the winds died
they read by the wave swell, by the birdflight,
by the phosphorescence a fathom under.

They were like children.

Of course, this chance to show what could be done on the
instrument was not to be overlooked.
I am a stag for swiftness, says the chief
I am a fort for shelter
I am a remedy for flatulence. 'Tell her
I am' the true wind.
I am a loyal servant
of the Democratic administration of this city.
I am a pocket watch.

The result was most gratifying . . . My dusky brother musician
cheerfully shared his 'poi' and canned salmon with me
thereafter. When we arrived at Honolulu . . . after a voyage of
thirty-four days, all but three of the castaways were sent to
the Marine Hospital. I was one of the robust ones thanks to
my musical friend

Its eyelid opens
and he snaps it shut.
Who are you, chief, between the tick
and tock?

I am a castaway by the albatross
I am a cracked skull in Odessa
I am a river on fire
I am innocent of all these charges.

> *if anyone asks*
> He tells the barman,
> *I'm not here.*

'ASSASSIN OF PRESIDENT McKINLEY AN ANARCHIST.
CONFESSES TO HAVING BEEN INCITED BY EMMA
GOLDMAN. WOMAN ANARCHIST WANTED.'

Grimoire

An intervening object does not impede the vision of the blessed . . .
Christ could see the face of his mother when she was prostrate on the
ground . . . as if he were looking directly at her face. It is clear that
the blessed can see the front of an object from the back, the face
through the back of the head.

Bartholomew Rimbertinus
On the Sensible Delights of Heaven, Venice, 1498

1

An afterlife in the theatre: 'And this, gentlemen (removes top of
skull), is the principal sulcus of the dorsolateral prefrontal cortex,
which manifests remarkable accord amongst the senses, even in the
sane. The smelling salts for Mr Bohman, Sister.'

2

To speak aloud among the sober of the sweet reek of bright green,
the soft hiss of yellow, the bitter shapes of the sound of the space in
which we speak, their lavender numbers tasting of sesame, is
indiscreet. Make sense. But only one sense at a time. To remark on
the silence breaking on the facets of a word the way light breaks
across an oilslick to the polyphonic iridescence of simultaneous
orgasm betrays one to the panicked guest whose eyes alert the host
across the room. Patience, children. Learn to hush your wonder.

Same again? Our hostess is engaged. She's grinding crystals finely on 'his jet shewstone' having borrowed overnight from the museum that black Aztec mirror John Dee used to talk to angels in their own tongue. She likes a bit of fun.

Someone's pounding on the door but she's caught her own gaze mid-sniff and is snagged in the talons of Quetzalcoatl, the feathered reptile trapped in the obsidian, twin god of self-reflection. She keeps to her knees as he tells her all she needs to know.

Keep up! The argument has run ahead, like an angry bearded black-robed bishop who leads us through a labyrinth of alleys to Chloras, goldsmith, busy through the night in his workshop of important toys. Here, a monk that kneels at clockwork prayer, here, a lady flautist trills and winks, and here, his masterpiece, that dragonfly of tin coil, springs and vermicelli gold. It tilts its head, it whirrs, it clicks its wings and – truly this the demon's work – it speaks: *Keep up! Reach out! Your day will come, Your fingers brush a face across the sea.*

5

At the commandment of the conjuror he dooth take awaie the sight of anie one. He is a great prince, taking the forme of a thrush, except he be brought to a chaulk triangle and therein he teacheth divinetie, rhetorike, logike, pyromancie. He giveth men the understanding of all birds, of the lowing of bullocks, and barking of dogs, and also of the sound and noise of waters, he ruleth now thirtie legions of divels who was of the celestiall orders and will possess agayne and rule the world.

6

Keep up. The argument will run ahead outstripping words, will tear down neural paths branching, sundering, recombining, out of sight and far beyond your power to direct. Upgraded man, inhaling sunlight, who listens in silence, who sees in the dark, what you might tell us of the world beyond speech no one, no, not even you, can say.

– IV –

*I slipped from my saddle in a dark courtyard
leaving my horse to the silent grooms*

ITALO CALVINO

Midriver

– and is a bridge: Now to either then:
child to lolly: spark across the wire:
lover to the target of desire:
Lambeth to Westminster: back again.
Verb's a vector not a monument,
but someone skipped a stone across this river
fixing its trajectory forever
in seven arches after the event
– so stops halfway and, neither there nor there,
but cold and rained on and intransitive,
watches London switch from *when* to *where*,
why to silence in the traffic jam,
thinks I can see the borough where I live
but here is temporarily who I am.

The River Glideth Of His Own Sweet Will

Who's this buck of eighteen come up the stairs
squinting from his *Rough Guide*
across the Thames into the late June sun
towards Lambeth, the wheel, the aquarium,

and St Thomas' Hospital where you lie
in the eighth-floor intensive-care unit
wired up to a heart monitor
staring north to Big Ben's crackled face?

But now the nurse pulls shut the blinds –
not that you'd have clocked one another.
What unaided eyes could possibly connect
thirty years across Westminster bridge
through traffic fumes, crowds,
children, career, marriage, mortgage?

Southwesternmost

I've a pocketwatch for telling space,
a compass tooled for reckoning by time,
to search this quadrant between six and nine
for traces of her song, her scent, her face.
Come night, that we might seek her there, come soon,
come shade the southwest quarter of this chart,
the damaged chamber of my mother's heart.

Mare Serenitatis on the moon,
this blindspot, tearhaze, cinder in the eye,
this cloudy star when I look left and down,
this corner of the crest without a crown,
this treeless plain where she went home to die.
I almost hear it now and hold its shape,
the famine song she's humming in my sleep.

Akhmatova Variations

No, he'd never leave us here alone.
He merely became an ear of grain,
the fine rain he sang into lines,
the shine struck from wet sand at low tide,
the bedside glass of water rippling,
the eye of a horse between two blinks,
or so we think, to console ourselves.
Hear that thunderous whisper?
It's time-lapse flowers bursting from the earth.
Years pass. At last, the echo fades
and the grasses kneel to a soundless wind
we insist on hearing as a prayer
shared by sisters of a silent order,
or those humblest of words, our names.

Where will I find you? Among the living
or pressed between my palms in prayer,
a shade swept like a leaf among shades?
I hereby dedicate to you the following:
First, my days, entire, and the delirious dawn
when the door of sleep clicks shut behind me,
the blue fire of my eyes, open, focused,
but still twitching like a dreamer's.
And all these too I offer up:
my unblemished sacrificial flock,
blank pages in a notebook in a locked drawer,
though no God could know me as well as you,
not my interrogator, not my torturer,
not even those who took, and forgot, my kiss.

If only you knew what trifles spark a poem.
A scream from the flat above
and you go cold hoping it's laughter.
That chill can kick-start the engine.
Or when you hang up and I hear clicks,
or clock the car drawn up beneath my window,
the punch in my chest is the muse touching my heart.
It's brazen, this art. A poet might clench her eyes,
might stand with her face to the wall, listening
for footsteps in the corridor, trying not to think,
and suddenly a line betrays itself.

Two lovers walk abroad, night-riddled and bereaved
because, years hence, some perfect stranger dreams they do
and dreams their every word of parting
but can't decide the colour of his eyes,
can't aim the loaded pistol of her gaze.
They walk the darkest alleyways because
their only freedom's in obscurity
(but tell me, is that stranger you or me?).

Now deep inside the dream the moon emerges
exposing us, and now our footsteps click
into their positions on a mandala.
My whisper is a tile in a mosaic,
the sky a spray of one-star constellations:
the pupil, the tear, the full stop.

As we sat in deathwatch on our love,
the wraith of our first days knocked on the door,
then forced it down. There spread the silver willow
in all its splendour ghosting over us.
How could we meet its gaze or bear to suffer
the birdsong bursting from its branches,
the song of how we'd die for one another?

Not grenadiers bleeding but your night bus leaving
Not falcons and gyres but discarded desires
Not the death of the tsar but the smell of fresh tar
Not theories of language but gunplay in marriage
Not the marble of wrath but your hair in my mouth

The New Grey

It's black, it says here, but not jet, not shiny,
more the charcoal-black old family snapshots burn,
the dark of the cathedral vault aswarm with pigeons
muted to an expensive almost-blue-black.
See a woman in black? See me touching her shoulder?
We weren't friends, but . . . But what? Hear my words
blow out like lamps in series down a mine shaft?
The colour of the coal dust rising up to gag me
is this new shade, exactly. Can we discuss this?
I need to get fluent in grey if I want to survive.
I need a job to earn enough to buy that shirt
in the same unsayable shade that hid in the wardrobe
in a room I woke in as a child.

The Swear Box

They open, at forty, cabinets their fathers locked,
boys again, whispering bad words beneath blankets,
girls spitting the big verbs at their mirrors.
Something sharp and rusty on their tongues again,
something more he'd hoped to spare them:
new bedside silences for visiting hours,
new definitions for never, for over.
quiet words boomed from pulpit mics,
and, afterwards, the whispers of dark-suited cousins.
Women hugging pregnant friends practice
new phrases, concealing the chill. Grown men
yank shut the curtains of their brilliant studies
to stop the black glass listening.

A Sicilian Defence

It is another story altogether
by lanternlight, beneath two birches
and the sound of a shallow river
where two men are playing chess
for as long as either will remember,
opening P–K4, P–QB4.
It's not a question of either/or –
one might be my father, or me at sixty.
The other might as well be me
thinking: his right's my left, my left
his right. I see it now in a different light.
I know it now by another name.

Is it any wonder then this game
runs on through this and every night
forever, lit by lanternlight, two birches
and the sound of a river?

Exile's End

You will do the very last thing.
Wait then for a noise in the chest,
between depth charge and gong,
like the seadoors slamming on the car deck.
Wait for the white noise and then cold astern.

Gaze down over the rim of the enormous lamp.
Observe the skilled frenzy of the physicians,
a nurse's bald patch, blood. These will blur,
as sure as you've forgotten the voices
of your childhood friends, or your toys.

Or, you may note with mild surprise,
your name. For the face they now cover
is a stranger's and it always has been.
Turn away. We commend you to the light,
Where all reliable accounts conclude.

Two Spells For Sleeping

Eight white stones
in a moonlit garden,
to carry her safe
across the bracken
on a gravel path
like a silvery ribbon
seven eels in the urge of water
a necklace in rhyme
to help her remember
a river to carry her
unheard laughter
to light about her
weary mirror
six candles for a king's daughter
five sighs for a drooping head
a prayer to be whispered
a book to be read
four ghosts to gentle her bed
three owls in the dusk falling
what is that name
you hear them calling?
In the soft dark welling,
two tales to be telling,
one spell for sleeping,
one for kissing,
for leaving.